The Life-Changing Magic of Tidying Up: The Japanese Art of Decluttering and Organizing

Summary and Analysis

By QuickRead

Contents

Introduction

Known as one of the most trusted guides when it comes to cleaning one's home, Marie Kondo's *The Life Changing Magic of Tidying Up* will really make it easy for you to clean, and organize your digs. It is also considered as one of Tokyo's most important phenomena that is also making its way to the world!

This is because of the so-called *KonMari Method,* a systematic and simplified way of keeping your place in check. What makes it different from other cleaning methods out there is that instead of asking the person to clean room by room, Kondo believes that it is better to clean and segregate by category. This, she believes, would lead to better and more efficient results.

Moreover, Kondo also happens to conduct meetings with clients, and personally helps them clean their homes. It is said that her waiting list is filled for up to three long months—or even more!

The book itself consists of 214 pages—and for some people, that is a little too long. That's why this book is created: to give you the gist of the book, help you understand Kondo's techniques, and help you strategize on how to clean and organize your home—without having to read the book itself, or be part of Kondo's unending waiting list!

What are you waiting for?

Read this book now, and find out how!

Chapter 1: Know What's Wrong

The first chapter of Kondo's book is entitled *Why Can't I Keep My House in Order?*

According to this chapter, the problem that most people encounter is that they haven't had the chance to create the framework of being responsible when it comes to cleaning their homes.

This mostly happens because people associate the act of cleaning to something that's not important, or something like a chore that they can always put off for later. You yourself may even remember cleaning as a form of manipulation, if not a punishment, from your parents. Of course, when you think this way, cleaning really becomes a drag.

You have to realize that cleaning starts from you—then, it will all flow from there.

Cleaning Marathons are not equal to Rebounds

One of the things that Marie Kondo believes is that the connotation that cleaning marathons causes rebounds are wrong.

She knows that over the years, there have been lots of articles pertaining to that matter. However, Kondo believes otherwise.

This is because she thinks that when you try to tidy up your house every single day, you are only allowing yourself to clean forever. This means you would not be able to save time, and instead just double your effort.

But, if you choose to think of cleaning as an event, you will see it as something special. This means that you have to set one special day for it and even dress up for the occasion in comfortable clothes, such as:

1. Loose shirts

2. Boots

3. Slippers

4. Shorts/ leggings

5. Sundresses

This way, you know that you're ready to clean, and you would not be thinking about anything else. Setting a weekend or two for cleaning would already be good.

Aiming for Perfection

Another thing that Kondo hates seeing in magazines and articles is how some writers tell people not to worry about perfection, and that they should just clean whatever they can, whenever they can.

This is wrong. Just like anything important in life, one must always aim for perfection. After all, you're the one who's going to still live in your house, and you are the one who will be using all the items you have there.

When you start aiming for perfection at home, everything else in your life would follow. Whatever you do in life, you will think of doing them at the best of your abilities, too. You wouldn't just settle for "Okay", or "Just Right"—you will always aim for the best; you will always aim to be the greatest.

The Moment You Start, You Reset Your Life

See, the problem with most people is that they don't think they could still aim for perfection because they're used to being second best, or they feel like they were not able—and would not be able—to beat other people.

Cleaning should then be your cue to start over again. Once you clean your space, you will have a refreshed, positive outlook in life. When you see that everything around you is clean, you also feel cleans and youthful inside—and it will definitely show.

Marie Kondo says that the act of cleaning should feel like a purge. No, you are not going to throw up, or kill people (just like in the movie of the same name), but you'll somehow be purging your soul through the act of throwing away what you no longer need, and keeping the things that matter in place. In short, you will purge your soul and become a new person by means of cleaning your house!

Sort by Category, Not Location

This is one of the most important points of the book. Kondo reiterates that the reason why cleaning does not become successful for most people is that they choose to clean by rooms, and not by categories.

See, what happens when you clean by location is that you tend to be extremely nostalgic, and so instead of moving on to another room, you just tend to stay in the room that you're in instead of moving on, and in the end, you don't get to clean anything. That is not what you want to happen.

So, Kondo reiterates that cleaning by category is the way to go. This means you have to sort items by type. For example: clothes, books, photos, papers, kitchenware, etc. This way, it would be so much easier for you to lay your items down, and see what you should keep, and what you should throw away.

Don't change methods to suit your personality

Another important thing to remember is that cleaning is not something that you can expect to fit with your personality.

If you want to be successful in cleaning your house, you have to follow what you'll read about in this book. Do not aim to be comfortable, or lousy. Always remember that you have to aim for perfection—because that is exactly what will lead you to success.

Chapter 2: Discard First

Now, let's move on to the second chapter of the book, which Kondo calls *Finish Discarding First.*

See, Kondo believes that in order to clean your house, you have to start discarding the things that you no longer need, and you have to do it all at once. This is because if you keep leaving things behind, and if you keep putting off discarding other things for tomorrow, you'll never be able to do any kind of cleaning at all.

But, if you allow yourself to start discarding now, you will be able to do more later. This isn't just about cleaning, you see. When you already get to clean your place—and clean up your act—everything else will flow naturally.

Visualize your destination

One of the things that could help you understand what you need to discard is having a vision about what you want to keep, and where exactly you need to go.

Some may think that it's crazy to think of a vision, given that for others cleaning is just a trivial thing, but the thing is that like everything else in life, you need to treat the act of cleaning as something special.

So, you do have to list down your vision first. It is said that it's important to ask yourself questions about this so that you can form your own vision. Sample questions include:

1. What makes the act of cleaning so important to you?

2. Why do you need to tidy up?

3. What do you think you could do to create more space at home?

4. How do you visualize your dream room to be?

5. Do you think your living room is presentable enough?

6. What keeps your bathroom dirty?

7. Why is your bedroom so shallow? Why don't you have enough space?

The key is to make sure that you ask yourself specific questions so that you also could give specific answers. For example:

1. Cleaning is important because in a way, it is a reflection of myself. If my house is not clean, I am not clean either—and that's definitely not something good.

2. I need to tidy up because my house is already in disarray and I no longer feel good any time I am home.

3. I think I need to start discarding what I no longer need. By doing this, I could free up more space at home, I could redecorate, and I definitely could make my house look better.

4. I want my room to resemble my personality; I'm going to change the wallpaper, redecorate with glow-in-the-dark icons, and put more paintings and ornaments. This would not happen with all the clutter around.

5. I don't think my living room is still presentable enough, and for this, I am ashamed. I know I need to clean up more or else, people would probably talk about it, and that's not something good.

6. All these old bottles of shampoo and body wash are keeping my bathroom in disarray; I need to throw them away.

7. My bedroom is shallow because I have all these clothes strewn on the floor, and my books have not been shelved properly, too.

Once you have created your vision, it will be easy for you to keep track of the items you have at home, and understand what you need to throw away.

Does it spark joy?

Another thing that you should keep in mind is to ask yourself whether the certain items you have at home still sparks joy inside whenever you see them.

While there are times when it's good to be nostalgic, most of the time, it only causes you to live in the past—and you always have to live in the present, and look forward to the future—not the other way around.

It would be helpful if you could make a list of the items you have, or simply look at them while they're scattered all over the floor, and see whether they make you happy or not. If they don't, don't be scared to chuck them out.

Remember to make room only for the things that matter—and nothing else.

One Category at a time

When it comes to putting things down on the floor, do it one category at a time. Again, this is essential.

Start with the clothes, then your books, CDs, accessories, other important documents, etc. Remember to clear one category first before the other so that it would be easy for you to throw away the things that you no longer need. Don't move on to another category without finishing one first—or else you'll create more of a mess.

Never start with mementos!

You probably already know why, don't you?

When you start with mementos, you do not become productive because you only end up associating memories with them. And even if you are no longer friends with the person who gave you those, you might end up feeling guilty about throwing them away. This is a big no-no!

Start with the important things first, so that when you see your mementos, you'll probably be a little too tired and you will make sensible decisions, instead of decisions based on how you feel.

Never clean when your family is around

Your family can prove to be a distraction because you don't really have the same things in mind. For example, a certain item no longer brings you joy, yet, your mother feels like you should still keep it because it was given to you by your childhood friend—one she believes is still your best friend, but apparently, you do not see eye to eye with this person anymore.

So, when you try to organize your things while your family is around, you just might feel confused. There may also be times when you try telling your family that you can clean up on your own, but then they'll just say that they want to help and the like. Eventually, what would happen is that you wouldn't be able to tidy up your house the way you want to, and this will make you resent your parents even more.

Furthermore, Kondo's studies also prove that sometimes, the reason why tension happens between you and your family is because of the state of your room, or of the house (if you have your own). If you live in a cluttered house, your mind would be cluttered, too.

When this happens, you tend to take out the stress on your family—and that is never really a good thing. So, make sure you tell them not to come around when you know you are going to clean, and to always remember that whatever you do not need, your family does not need either! Never feel guilty about throwing away those that you no longer like just because your family asks you to keep them.

It is a dialogue with one's self

Tidying is a means of introspection. It is a chance to get to know yourself better again, and understand who you are right now—and not who you were back then. It is a way of understanding what is important at the moment.

Sure, something may have meant much to you back then, but you have to understand whether or not it is still good for you today. When you clean up alone, you wouldn't feel like you have to conform to the likes of others, and that you would not have to explain why you want to keep or throw the items that you have.

By tidying up, you get to help yourself get a better disposition in life, and you begin to feel like you can be whoever you want to be.

What to do when you can't throw something away

There is always the struggle of not being able to throw something away because you feel like you might still use it in the future. Or, you feel like it's a part of your past and it has to stay with you.

The thing with life is that it always changes. You can never expect it to stay the same, and the more you do that, the more disappointed you'll be.

The problem with people is that they often have a hard time letting go. They don't know how to put a wall between the past and the present, and thus, they just continue hoarding until they no longer have space for the things that matter. Do you want to be one of those people? Of course not.

Deep down, you know you could be a better person if you know how to keep only the things you need, and discard those that you no longer do. Think about the space you could get after throwing those things away. Think about how dirty those things are already, and why it's okay to throw them away. Think about getting a clean slate, and feeling renewed. Think about other things you could buy because you freed up some space.

This could only lead you to better things, so stop looking back and remember that you are tidying up for your future!

Chapter 3: The Magic of Tidying by Category

The next thing that the book talk about is how you should tidy categorically and in the right order. Interestingly, the author shares a story of how some of her clients would talk to her in such a way that they have extreme fear about cleaning their homes. Some would even ask her about how one could clean house in a short amount of time, or if it's really possible to get rid of the clutter.

The answer is of course, yes. No matter how crappy you think your house is, there's still hope for it—especially if you believe in it.

The reason why most people are intimidated about the idea of cleaning is because of the fact that they feel like there's so much clutter already and they have no idea how and where to start. If you've been reading this analysis, you probably already have an idea about what needs to be done: Tidying categorically, of course.

Have you heard of the saying that one should break down his goals in order for the said goals to come true? Well, that works for tidying up your house, too. You have to make sure that you sort the categories into smaller ones. You will learn more about this below.

Clothing

For clothes, Marie Kondo believes that you have to segregate them into the following categories:

- Shirts, sweaters, and other tops

- Skirts, trousers, and other bottoms

- Suits, coats, jackets, and clothes that should be hung

- Underwear

- Socks

- Clothes for specific events, such as uniforms, formal wear, swimsuits, etc.

- Hats, belts, scarves, and other hosiery

- Shoes

Now, what you have to do is put down all of your clothes on the floor, and then segregate them into the aforementioned categories. Make sure that you really get them all out and you leave nothing behind. This way, you could really have them separated, and get to throw what you do not need anymore.

Basically, the author believes that you have to ask yourself two questions that will help you decide whether a piece of clothing needs to be kept or not. These questions are:

1. Do you actually like seeing that piece of clothing, or would you rather not see it again?, and;

2. Would you be able to wear it again? When and how do you think?

See, those are really simple questions that most people fail to ask themselves. But now that you know, it's best that you never forget because they'd help you fix your life for the better.

Folding the Clothes

Folding your clothes would be better, too, according to the author. She said that it helps you minimize things, and give you more space in your room. It would also give your clothes longer shelf life, and you can organize them based on the categories above. Of course, you have to hang clothes that originally need to be hung, but otherwise, you should work on the rest of your clothes. You have to fold your clothes into rectangles because those would fit best in your closet, and would give the idea that the clothes are "light"—so they wouldn't take up too much space, and wouldn't make you feel heavy, at all.

Incidentally, the act of folding coincides with this Japanese healing method called *Te-Ate*, which means "to heal". Once you put your hands on them, you will feel better when you wear them—at least that's what Kondo believes in. So, in a way, you're not just cleaning out your closet, you're also giving yourself the chance to feel better again.

Don't think about "Seasonal Clothes"

Kondo believes that people shouldn't arrange clothes seasonally, because these days, one could wear almost anything because of thermostat and air-conditioning options. One only has to buy clothes that he knows he'd be able to use for the rest of the year, instead of buying clothes that he'd probably only wear once.

You probably notice that the author is generalizing here, but you could also keep in mind that she's probably talking about the innovations in Japan, which is her country of origin. Maybe, you could just remind yourself to buy clothes that would work well for the weather in your country—so you wouldn't have to fix by season.

Books

As for books, the categories you have to follow are:

1. Books that you read for pleasure

2. Cookbooks, how-to's, informational, and other forms of references

3. Coffee table books, photography books, etc.

4. Magazines

The author says that you also have to lay all your books down on the floor, and then sort them out. Of course, you have to make sure that you've taken anti-histamines or anything that could fend off allergies if you know that some of your books are pretty dusty already.

Now, don't fall into the trap of reading while you clean. This would only make you feel nostalgic and would make it hard for you to continue what you're doing. Focus on tidying up.

Speaking of not reading books, you know, you have those books that you say you will read some other time, right? The thing is, there is a 90% chance that you would end up not reading them at all. So the best thing to do is make sure that you discard them, or just give them away. But, don't ever think of still keeping them in your shelves, okay?

Papers

When it comes to papers, make sure that you discard EVERYTHING: receipts, scratch papers, drafts, etc. Unless the paper is extremely important (i.e., birth certificates, social security forms, etc.), you have to throw them away.

As for important papers, the key is to make sure that you know where to keep them. Try using folders or clear files, and the like.

Komono

Komono is a term given to miscellaneous items, such as jewelries, or mementos. Marie Kondo's key rule here is to make sure that you only keep those that you can use, and those that you still like. Do not keep something just because you got it from the wedding ceremony of your oldest friend, or because it has been with you for so long. At this stage, you should already be able to let go of that way of thinking, you know?

There are also disposable komonos, such as plastic cups, and the like. Remember it would not be right to still keep these things around. They do not do anything good for you, or for your house, which means that they definitely should go!

Small Change

Another problem that most people have is that they keep on putting their loose change all around the house, instead of keeping the change in their pockets.

Marie Kondo believes that in order to clear the house of loose change, you have to keep the mantra of keeping small change in your pocket, instead of putting them wherever you think you could.

Photos

Ah, this one is tricky.

According to Kondo, when it comes to keeping photos, you only have to keep those that resemble who you are now. After all, you can always just scan old photos, and keep them online, but you really do not have to keep hard copies with you.

The author believes that it's always best to just keep photos that show who you are at the moment so that you can focus on this part of your life, instead of anything else. Remember that you have to live in the now, and not in yesterday or so.

Always remember to cherish who you are now. That is the only thing that matters.

Reduce until you are content

Another tip that Kondo shares is that you just have to keep on reducing the piles of things you have at home until you feel right.

There would always be that moment when you feel like, hey, you were able to clean up the house the way you wanted to. When that happens, stop what you are doing, look around you, and check whether you feel right about the house. If you do, you'll know you have done the right thing.

Plus, the author also believes that it is important for you to follow your intuition. By doing this, you are leading yourself to a right place, and you will surely be able to clean up your house and make it look perfect!

Chapter 4: Store Things and Make Life Shine

The fourth chapter of the book is all about the power of storing things properly. It is said that doing so will definitely make your life shine, and make you feel so much better about yourself.

A Place for Everything

The number 1 thing you have to keep in mind is that there has to be a place for every single thing you decide to keep, so that none of them would be laying around the house with nowhere to go.

For example:

- Gowns, long dresses, dress robes, formal wear should be hung in the closet;
- Rubber shoes should occupy the 2nd space of the shoe rack;
- Flip-flops and sandals should occupy the lowest rack;
- Formal shoes should be on top;
- T-shirts and other clothing items must be folded and segregated based on the occasion where they could be used;
- Favorite books should be on a shelf where you could easily reach them;

- Text books should all come together, and be near your study area so you could easily use them for reviewing;

- Novels should be segregated based on category. You might also want to label their place in the shelves;

- Mementos should be displayed on a single shelf, or in a part of the house where you feel they work best;

- Accessories should be in tin holders and the like, etc.

Of course, this is just an example. Segregate the way you see fit, but only do it once you're done discarding the things that you no longer need.

Pursue Simplicity

The author also shares that when it comes to storage, you should always pursue simplicity. This means your things do not have to be scattered, but should be kept in such a way that you will easily know where they are.

Incidentally, this is linked to a minimalist approach of cleaning, which has always been praised as one of the most effective means of keeping a house in tip-top shape.

So, why exactly should you go for simplicity? Here are a couple good reasons:

1. You get to create room for what's important. You no longer have to deal with the clutter around you, or have a hard time finding one simple object because you already know where it would be.

2. You get to focus on other things in your life. You wouldn't have to spend time cleaning the house every single day anymore, and you could make time to become more skilled, and enjoy your hobbies, instead of not having time for them because you have to clean up.

3. You get to feel free! It's such a cliché, but it's true. A minimalist approach would easily make you feel like you have nothing to worry about, which would definitely lead to your peace of mind and sense of security. It is an old belief that when you feel at peace in your surroundings, it will also be easy for you to feel at peace with yourself, and therefore, you wouldn't feel bound by your past. It would be easy for you to take hold of opportunities that would make you grow!

In a sense, cleaning your house and using a minimalist approach for your storage would help you gain better things in life—and that is for sure!

Things you should forget

Kondo believes that in order to tidy your house well, you have to forget about frequency of use, and flow planning, amongst other things.

Some people believe that you have to keep frequently used items together so that it would be easy for you to grab hold of them whenever you need them, but the thing is that this only provides you with more clutter. Imagine a comb sitting with a book. Or, toothbrushes near your favorite mug! Yikes!

See, when you think of storing things based on frequency of use, mess just starts piling up. This means you'll be back to square one, and that is never a good thing.

It is also said that you do not have to buy items just because they're new, or they're the current fad. You know, fads always fade, and you should not pressure yourself into buying and keeping things just because everybody else has them, too.

Remember to buy and keep only what you need. That's the general rule of this book!

Let's talk about your bag

Now, your bag is something important. It holds things that are dear to you, simply because you use these things every day, or whenever you need to go somewhere.

According to Kondo, it's imperative that you empty your bag every day. Sure, you may be a little too lazy to do this, but the thing is that it will somehow make you realize that if you can clean a single item as your bag daily, you would not have a hard time cleaning your house the way you should.

You should definitely rid your bag off the things you may have put there and should not be there, such as receipts, candy wrappers, and other pieces of paper. You don't need those in your bag, or with you, in any way. Remember that clutter won't lead to good things.

Another key to bag storage is to make sure that you store smaller bags in bigger ones. This way, you would not have a hard time keeping all your bags together, and you won't have to find places to store them in the house.

If they're on the floor, they have to be inside the closet

This is one of the easiest tips in the book. If you see things scattered on the floor, and if they're not adding any aesthetic purpose in the house, take it upon yourself to keep them in the closest—or wherever storage box you see fit.

Keep things out of the bath and kitchen sink

One habit that most people have is they usually keep knick-knacks on the kitchen and bathroom sinks. This is not good because it only adds to the clutter at home.

People often unwittingly take up the annoying habit of keeping plastic soap and shampoo bottles even if they're really no longer going to use them. When this happens, the clutter in the bathroom just becomes so unmanageable, and the worst part is that people would still think it is normal.

And then when it comes to the kitchen sink, people often have those condiments at bay. Sometimes, knives are easily seen, too. And then there is the fact that some people just fail to wash their dishes right away and so there gets to be a stack of dirty dishes in the sink—which makes the sink so dirty, it becomes annoying.

So, take it upon yourself to wash the dishes right away. Just like your other responsibilities, those dishes would not really go away unless you clean them. And once you clean them, your sink would no longer look miserable—and you can set forth to segregate and arrange the other items in the kitchen, too.

The top shelf is your personal shrine

Another easy way to make sure that your shelves won't get cluttered is to make sure that the top shelf should be considered as your "Personal Shrine". This means that whatever feels closest to you as a person, and whatever makes your heart happy should be kept in there.

Why?

Well, it's simply because Kondo believes that people often find it easy to keep a space clean when they know the things they love are there. It's the same as being easily protective of the people you know and love, you know? When you know that you love someone, your instinct tells you to protect this person at all costs, and keep the relationship as perfect as could be.

That should also be your mantra when it comes to your top shelf. Keep things that are important to you, such as your favorite books, frame typography of your favorite lyrics, some mementos, the best photo you have right now, etc. Once you keep the top shelf in order, you'll see how easy it would be for you to keep the rest of the shelves looking their best, too!

Decorate closet with secret delights

According to most people who have read Marie Kondo's book, one of the best things they have learned from the book is the importance of decorating one's closet with her secret delights.

This means you have to treat your closet as if it is a room. You can put a couch, a beanbag, some trinkets, some stuffed toys, maybe even a book or two. Or, you could paint the inside of your closet with your favorite colors. Decorate it with stickers. Or, paint one side with a certain color and then keep same-colored items in the said side of your closet. You see, the possibilities are endless!

By being creative in decorating your closet, you would no longer be too lazy in cleaning it again next time. You might even have fun making sure that it looks presentable and photogenic, just like most celebrities' closets are.

When you open your closet and see how beautiful it is, you would no longer feel like clothes should just be strewn all around the floor. You would no longer feel lazy about dressing up. You would treat the act of dressing up as something special—and Kondo wants you to feel that way about everything in your life, even cleaning up!

Unpack and de-tag new clothes immediately

Quick: See if you can answer these questions:

1. Are there still clothes that are in their plastic bags in the house?
2. Do you still have some clothes with tags on?

3. Are some of the items you have shopped for in the past couple of weeks still unpacked?

If your answer to any of these is *Yes,* then it means you have not been cleaning up properly!

And why is that so?

Well, it's probably just because you are too tired from shopping. But, what about tomorrow? Would you still consider yourself tired?

Again, this all boils down to one's laziness in unpacking things. Instead of keeping those things in order, they only end up on the floor, or on certain parts of the closet, unused and unappreciated.

Remember that you have to treat your items as if they have feelings. You have to be thankful that they're around, and one of the ways of doing that is make sure they get used. Now, this can only be done if you choose to unpack and un-tag them right away, instead of waiting for months or years before you even lay a hand on them!

This way, it would also be easy for you to dispose the packaging of those items so they would not add up to the clutter in your house. Easy, isn't it?

Written Noise

So, you're now probably thinking: *What in the world is Written Noise?!*

Written Information basically applies to whatever's written on the items you have at home: labels, receipts, words written on cups or mugs, etc.

Sometimes, they're part of the aesthetics. But other times, they just somehow make you feel contrived and unhappy. This is because they add to the negativity in your head, which is never really a good thing.

What you can do here is peel off those things that strike you as too bright or just not right. You have the right to do that, you see?

According to Kondo, written noise not only adds to clutter at home, it also adds to the mess in your head. So, make it a point to take them off, and replace them with photos of beautiful things, instead. Try to write positive quotes and stick them where you could easily see them. Don't let your life be bound by all the negative things you see.

Appreciate your possessions

Marie Kondo says that you should always learn how to appreciate your possessions, because it's a reflection of your ability to appreciate whatever you have around you. When you do this, your life becomes a harmonious thread of experiences, and you would no longer have a hard time dealing with your problems.

Incidentally, this is also linked to the thought that what you appreciate also begins to appreciate you. Plus, there's the fact that it is okay to buy and store things as long as they make you happy. Sometimes, this could be therapeutic.

For example:

1. Saying thank you because you got to buy food that you have been craving for after a long, hard day at work. In turn, this will help you be more motivated at work, so you'll be able to give the best of your abilities and do work that's profitable, not only for you, but also for your bosses.

2. Being thankful that you're able to arrange your clothes by color or by occasion. This will make you feel like dressing up could actually be fun!

3. Making space for hot shower in your bathroom. This will make you see that it was good you kept your bathroom clean because now, bathing time would be even better!

When you see that the things around you are not just things but are actually important in keeping your life in check, life would be so much lighter and happier! You would no longer feel alone because you'll understand that the items you have are important in making your life work the way it is supposed to. You would then be more appreciative of other things in your life, and thus, you will realize that keeping things in order is actually not a problem!

Chapter 5: Tidying Dramatically Transforms Your Life!

Finally, you have reached the last chapter of the book—and what you should know about it.

According to the author, the Life Changing Magic of Tidying is the fact that it dramatically transforms your life. Here's why.

You get to know what you want

As mentioned earlier, there are times that the stress you feel and the state of your mind are all connected to how untidy your house is.

But, some light and clarity happens when you begin to see past the surface; when you take away the things that you do not need and keep only those that are important to you and the growth of your soul.

The magic happens because you get to understand who you are now, as opposed to who you were--because there is actually a vast difference between yesterday and today. Even if something meant a lot to you yesterday, there might be something inside that says "No, don't keep that anymore" today. And that's normal.

It is not about being fickle-minded, you see. It's more of allowing yourself the chance to see the world in a new light; one where you would no longer have to conform to others—which means that you're finally confident about who you are.

Gaining confidence and losing anxiety

The simple act of throwing away things that you no longer need is a big sign of confidence.

Why?

Well, because there are some people who actually could not let go of clutter just because they feel like they'd be losing part of themselves once they do that. In reality, clinging on to old things that are already broken is just a reflection that one is still holding on tight to the past.

Is it wrong to be nostalgic and sentimental?

Of course not. But you don't have to let your decisions be affected by certain items that no longer should be in your life, but you feel compelled to let stay there. Kondo says that there is nothing wrong about letting go, because there are a lot of lessons that you can learn once you begin to let go.

Some of these include:

1. Knowing that you are actually your own person, and that you do not have to be defined by the things and people around you;

2. Knowing that the future is actually in your hands, and that you have the power to turn your life around;

3. Knowing that there is a certain kind of freedom that comes with letting go.

Again, you'll only figure these things out when you allow yourself to clean up—not when you just allow yourself to get stuck.

In life, it's not just about gaining; letting go is also just as important—you always have to remember that.

Greet your house

Kondo also says that one of the ways for the whole magic of tidying to work is to make sure that you do not forget greeting your house.

For example, after a long day outside and upon opening the door, you should say *Thank heavens I'm home,* or *I'm so glad to be home,* or *Home sweet home* instead of just blurting out profanities about how exhausting your day was, or that you just wish you were asleep the whole day.

As Kondo says, your living space actually affects the state of your body. When you tell your house that you're always just so exhausted and that you do not like your life, which vibes do you think it would give you back?

As mentioned earlier, you have to appreciate the things around you, and of course, this includes your house. Just put yourself in your house's shoes. It gets all the frustrations and negative vibes that you have, so while there, you probably just feel like it's doing no good for you, when the real issue is that you're the one who's doing nothing to help make it amazing.

Treat your house with kindness. Treat it the way you would the beautiful surroundings you see. Your house is your home and it deserves all of your love and respect.

Tidying increases good fortune

The author says that while her book was not purely based on Feng Shui, or the Chinese Philosophical System of Harmony, she also believes that the two could come together.

You see, Feng Shui deals a lot with positioning of items. It is said that certain positions mean good luck, while others mean bad luck—which you should change.

Now, you won't be able to arrange those pieces in a harmonious and systematic manner if you do not tidy up your place, to begin with. When you tidy up, you begin to see all the things that have probably been caught up in the rubble for so long—and so you get to begin the process of rearranging them to catch good vibes!

Then again, it still starts with you. If you don't believe in good luck, and if you do not treat your house properly, none of your schemes would work.

Identify what's precious

You do not need Golum or Smigel to tell you what is *Your Precious*—you can do that by yourself.

Again, it all goes back to the fact that you only have to keep things that spark joy; that make you feel good about yourself, and that spark some fire in your heart. Those are the things that are part of your existence.

These may include:

1. Things that make you joyful—something you feel deep inside, and not just the fleeting, fading kind of happiness;

2. Things that remind you of who you really are—the person you have envisioned, the person innate to you, and not what others deem you to be;

3. Things that remind you of your dreams—and that push you to do something to get them, or;

4. Things that make you smile, simply, without other things getting into your head.

And as for everything else?

Well, you can let them go. Just choose to be surrounded by things that spark joy, and you'll see that everything will feel so much better—and that you'll be compelled to clean up, and follow your dreams.

When you are surrounded by things that spark joy, you get into this place of confidence and security. You get to appreciate who you really are, and you will realize that you are doing the right thing!

Let your real life begin

How many times have you felt like you're not living your own life? Like, you're not happy, and you just want to live somebody else's life?

It's not the nicest kind of feeling, is it?

When you get to understand that letting go of clutter is important, and that tidying would change your life for the better, you are allowing yourself to live the kind of life you want—your real life, that is!

So, after reading this book, apply what you have learned, put your house in order, and surely, your life will be in order, too!

You just have to start—and it will all flow smoothly!

Conclusion

Thank you for reading this book!

I hope that with the help of this summary, you have learned what Marie Kondo's Life Changing Magic of Tidying is all about.

Remember, the Konmari method is all about:

1. Discarding what you don't need
2. Keeping things in order
3. Giving everything a place to stay in
4. Making sure your house is tidy

Make sure that you apply what you have learned into your life, and you will definitely see some positive changes!

Finally, if you enjoyed this book, please take time to post a review on Amazon. It will be greatly appreciated.

Thank you, and good luck!

13463316R00027

Printed in Great Britain
by Amazon.co.uk, Ltd.,
Marston Gate.